# JONATHAN HARRIS

# Take Advantage of Section 8

*A Comprehensive Guide to Buying a Home*

Copyright © 2024 by Jonathan Harris

All rights reserved. No part of this publication may be reproduced, stored or transmitted in any form or by any means, electronic, mechanical, photocopying, recording, scanning, or otherwise without written permission from the publisher. It is illegal to copy this book, post it to a website, or distribute it by any other means without permission.

Jonathan Harris asserts the moral right to be identified as the author of this work.

Jonathan Harris has no responsibility for the persistence or accuracy of URLs for external or third-party Internet Websites referred to in this publication and does not guarantee that any content on such Websites is, or will remain, accurate or appropriate.

First edition

This book was professionally typeset on Reedsy.
Find out more at reedsy.com

# Contents

| | | |
|---|---|---|
| 1 | Chapter 1 | 1 |
| 2 | Chapter 2 | 2 |
| 3 | Chapter 3 | 4 |
| 4 | Chapter 4 | 7 |
| 5 | Chapter 5 | 9 |
| 6 | Chapter 6 | 11 |
| 7 | Chapter 7 | 13 |
| 8 | Chapter 8 | 15 |
| 9 | Chapter 9 | 17 |
| 10 | Chapter 10 | 19 |
| 11 | Chapter 11 | 21 |
| 12 | Chapter 12 | 23 |
| 13 | Chapter 13 | 25 |
| 14 | Chapter 14 | 27 |
| 15 | Chapter 15 | 29 |
| 16 | Chapter 16 | 32 |
| 17 | Chapter 17 | 34 |

# 1

## Chapter 1

Introduction

Welcome to your comprehensive guide on buying a home using Section 8 benefits. This eBook will provide you with detailed steps, tips, and essential information needed to navigate the process of transitioning from a renter to a homeowner under the Section 8 Homeownership Program. Homeownership is a significant milestone and this guide aims to empower you with the knowledge and resources to achieve this goal.

# 2

# Chapter 2

Understanding Section 8 Homeownership

*What is Section 8?*

Section 8, also known as the Housing Choice Voucher Program, is a federal program administered by the U.S. Department of Housing and Urban Development (HUD). It assists low-income families, the elderly, and the disabled in affording safe, decent, and sanitary housing in the private market. Participants receive housing vouchers that cover a portion of their rent based on their income and family size.

*Overview of the Section 8 Homeownership Program*

The Section 8 Homeownership Program allows eligible voucher recipients to use their housing assistance for homeownership rather than renting. This initiative aims to provide a pathway to homeownership for low-income families, helping them build

CHAPTER 2

equity and stabilize their living situations. Participants can use their vouchers to cover mortgage payments and other home-ownership expenses, such as property taxes and insurance.

# 3

# Chapter 3

Eligibility Requirements

*First-time Homebuyer Status*

To qualify for the Section 8 Homeownership Program, you must be a first-time homebuyer. A first-time homebuyer is defined as someone who has not owned a home in the past three years. Exceptions to this rule include:

- **Displaced Homemakers**: Individuals who have only owned a home with a spouse and are displaced due to divorce, domestic violence, or other qualifying circumstances.
- **Single Parents**: Individuals who have only owned a home with a former spouse while married and now have custody of one or more children.

This requirement ensures that the program targets those most in need of assistance in transitioning to homeownership.

*Income Requirements*

Your income must meet the minimum level set by your local PHA. Generally, this requirement is not less than the federal minimum wage multiplied by 2,000 hours. For example, if the federal minimum wage is $7.25 per hour, your annual income would need to be at least $14,500. However, these requirements may vary by PHA, and some may have higher income thresholds.

- **Exceptions for Elderly or Disabled Families**: If you are elderly or disabled, the income requirement may be waived or adjusted to accommodate your circumstances. Elderly families typically include households where the head, spouse, or sole member is 62 years of age or older.

*Employment Requirements*

At least one adult in the household must be employed full-time for at least a year before applying for the program. Full-time employment is usually defined as working at least 30 hours per week. This requirement ensures that families have a stable income to manage mortgage payments and other homeownership costs.

- **Exceptions for Elderly or Disabled Families**: If you are elderly or disabled, the employment requirement is waived. This acknowledges that individuals in these categories may have fixed incomes, such as Social Security benefits, that

TAKE ADVANTAGE OF SECTION 8

can support homeownership.

# 4

# Chapter 4

## Getting Started with Your Local PHA

*Finding Your Local PHA*

Your local Public Housing Authority (PHA) administers the Section 8 program. To find your local PHA:

- **Visit the HUD Website**: The HUD website provides a directory of PHAs across the country. You can search by state and city to find contact information for your local office.
- **Contact HUD Directly**: If you have difficulty finding your local PHA, you can contact HUD directly for assistance. They can provide you with the necessary information to get in touch with your PHA.

## Applying for the Section 8 Homeownership Program

Once you locate your local PHA, follow these steps to apply for the Section 8 Homeownership Program:

- **Contact the PHA**: Reach out to your PHA to express your interest in the homeownership program. Not all PHAs offer this program, so it's essential to confirm its availability.
- **Submit an Application**: If the program is available, you will need to submit an application. This may include providing documentation of your income, employment status, and other relevant information.
- **Attend an Orientation**: Some PHAs require applicants to attend an orientation session to learn more about the program and its requirements.
- **Receive Approval**: After reviewing your application, the PHA will determine your eligibility. If approved, you can begin the process of finding a home and securing financing.

# Chapter 5

## Homeownership Counseling

### Importance of Counseling

Homeownership counseling is a critical component of the Section 8 Homeownership Program. It prepares you for the responsibilities of owning a home and provides essential skills and knowledge to ensure long-term success. Counseling covers various topics, including financial management, home maintenance, and navigating the mortgage process.

## Topics Covered in Counseling

- **Budgeting and Financial Literacy**: Learn how to create and manage a budget, understand credit scores and reports, and develop strategies for saving money. Financial literacy is vital for maintaining stable homeownership.
- **Home Maintenance**: Gain knowledge about routine home maintenance tasks, such as plumbing, electrical work, and HVAC systems. Understanding basic home repairs can save money and prevent costly issues.
- **Mortgage Financing**: Learn about different types of mortgages, interest rates, and the home buying process. Understanding how to choose the right mortgage and negotiate terms is crucial.
- **Home Search Process**: Get tips on finding a suitable home within your budget, working with real estate agents, and negotiating purchase prices. This section also covers how to identify red flags during the home search.

# 6

# Chapter 6

Finding a Lender

*Approved Lenders*

Not all lenders are familiar with the Section 8 Homeownership Program, so it's essential to find a lender who participates. Your PHA can provide a list of approved lenders who have experience working with Section 8 voucher recipients.

- **Research and Compare**: Look for lenders with competitive interest rates and favorable loan terms. Compare different lenders to find the best fit for your financial situation.
- **Pre-Qualification Process**: Getting pre-qualified for a mortgage helps you understand how much you can afford. During pre-qualification, the lender reviews your income, credit history, and other financial information to provide

an estimate of the loan amount you qualify for.

## *Pre-Qualification Process*

- **Documentation**: Gather necessary documents, such as proof of income, tax returns, bank statements, and employment verification. These documents are required for the pre-qualification process.
- **Credit Check**: The lender will check your credit score and history to assess your financial health. A higher credit score can result in better loan terms.
- **Pre-Qualification Letter**: Once pre-qualified, the lender will provide a letter stating the estimated loan amount. This letter can be used when making offers on homes to show sellers you are a serious buyer.

# 7

# Chapter 7

Searching for a Home

*HUD Housing Standards*

The home you purchase must meet HUD's minimum property standards to ensure it is safe, sanitary, and decent. These standards include:

- **Structural Integrity**: The home must be structurally sound with no significant defects.
- **Plumbing and Electrical Systems**: All plumbing and electrical systems must be in good working order.
- **Safety Features**: The home must have working smoke detectors, safe access, and egress, and meet local safety codes.
- **Habitable Space**: The home must provide adequate living space for your family size.

*Setting a Budget*

Determine a realistic budget based on your pre-qualification amount and other financial factors. Consider the following when setting your budget:

- **Monthly Mortgage Payments**: Include principal, interest, taxes, and insurance (PITI) in your budget.
- **Upfront Costs**: Account for the down payment, closing costs, and any immediate repairs or upgrades needed.
- **Ongoing Expenses**: Factor in utilities, maintenance, and unexpected repair costs.

*Choosing the Right Neighborhood*

When searching for a home, consider the following factors to choose the right neighborhood:

- **School Districts**: If you have children, research the quality of local schools.
- **Safety**: Check crime rates and neighborhood safety statistics.
- **Proximity to Work**: Consider commute times and access to public transportation.
- **Amenities**: Look for nearby amenities such as parks, grocery stores, and healthcare facilities.

# 8

# Chapter 8

## Applying for a Mortgage

### Mortgage Assistance

Your Section 8 voucher can be used to cover mortgage-related expenses, making homeownership more affordable. Here's how the assistance works:

- **Voucher Payments**: The PHA will determine the amount of assistance based on your income and the mortgage payment amount. This assistance helps reduce your out-of-pocket expenses.
- **Eligible Expenses**: In addition to the principal and interest on the mortgage, voucher payments can cover property taxes, homeowner's insurance, mortgage insurance, and utility allowances.

## Down Payment Assistance

Some PHAs offer programs to help with the down payment and closing costs. Check with your PHA to see if you qualify for any of these programs:

- **Grants**: Some PHAs provide grants that do not need to be repaid.
- **Deferred Loans**: These loans are typically repaid when you sell the home or refinance the mortgage.
- **Matched Savings Programs**: Also known as Individual Development Accounts (IDAs), these programs match your savings for a down payment.

# 9

# Chapter 9

Closing the Sale

*Home Inspection*

A thorough home inspection is crucial to ensure the property is in good condition. Here's what to expect:

- **Hire a Qualified Inspector**: Choose a certified home inspector to assess the property's condition.
- **Inspection Report**: The inspector will provide a detailed report on the home's structure, systems, and any necessary repairs.
- **Negotiations**: Use the inspection report to negotiate repairs or price reductions with the seller.

## Appraisal Process

An appraisal is required by the lender to ensure the home's value supports the loan amount. Here's how it works:

- **Lender Orders Appraisal**: The lender will hire an appraiser to evaluate the property's market value.
- **Appraisal Report**: The appraiser will provide a report detailing the home's value based on comparable sales and market conditions.
- **Loan Approval**: The loan amount may be adjusted based on the appraised value.

## Closing Costs

Closing costs include various fees and expenses associated with finalizing the home purchase. Be prepared for the following:

- **Loan Origination Fees**: Charges by the lender for processing the loan.
- **Title Insurance**: Protects against claims on the property's title.
- **Recording Fees**: Charges for recording the deed with the local government.
- **Prepaid Expenses**: Includes homeowner's insurance, property taxes, and mortgage interest.

# 10

# Chapter 10

Post-Purchase Requirements

*Ongoing Compliance*

To continue receiving assistance, you must comply with ongoing requirements set by the PHA:

- **Annual Re-examinations**: The PHA will review your income and household composition annually to ensure you still qualify for assistance.
- **Home Inspections**: Periodic inspections by the PHA to ensure the property remains in good condition.

## Home Maintenance

Maintaining your home is essential for preserving its value and ensuring a safe living environment:

- **Routine Maintenance**: Regularly check and maintain systems such as HVAC, plumbing, and electrical.
- **Repairs**: Address any repairs promptly to prevent further damage.
- **Upkeep**: Keep the property clean and well-maintained.

## Financial Management

Effective financial management is key to successful homeownership:

- **Budgeting**: Continue to follow a budget that accounts for mortgage payments, utilities, maintenance, and other expenses.
- **Savings**: Build an emergency fund to cover unexpected repairs or financial setbacks.
- **Debt Management**: Avoid taking on excessive debt that could jeopardize your ability to make mortgage payments.

# 11

# Chapter 11

## Tips for Success

### Staying Informed

Keep yourself informed about your rights and responsibilities as a homeowner and Section 8 participant:

- **Regular Updates**: Stay in touch with your PHA for updates on program requirements and changes.
- **Community Resources**: Utilize community resources, such as local housing agencies and non-profits, for additional support and information.

### Budgeting Tips

Effective budgeting can help you manage your finances and avoid financial stress:

- **Track Expenses**: Regularly track your income and expenses to identify areas where you can save.
- **Prioritize Needs**: Focus on essential expenses, such as mortgage payments and utilities, before discretionary spending.
- **Review and Adjust**: Periodically review your budget and make adjustments as needed to stay on track.

*Seeking Additional Assistance*

Take advantage of additional resources and programs to support your homeownership journey:

- **Local Government Programs**: Many local governments offer programs to assist with home repairs, energy efficiency improvements, and property taxes.
- **Non-Profit Organizations**: Non-profits such as Habitat for Humanity and NeighborWorks America offer homeownership support and resources.
- **Financial Counseling**: Consider working with a financial counselor to improve your financial literacy and manage your budget effectively.

# 12

## Chapter 12

### Conclusion

Buying a home using Section 8 assistance is a detailed process that requires careful planning and adherence to program requirements. By following this comprehensive guide, you can navigate the path to homeownership with confidence and success. Remember to utilize the resources available to you, stay informed, and manage your finances wisely. With dedication and effort, you can achieve the dream of homeownership and enjoy the stability and security it brings.

TAKE ADVANTAGE OF SECTION 8

# 13

# Chapter 13

## DISPUTEBEE

*DisputeBee simplifies credit repair by automating the dispute process and providing easy-to-use tools. Here's how it helps:*

*Benefits*

*Automated Disputes: Quickly generate and send dispute letters to credit bureaus.*

*User-Friendly: Designed for ease of use, even for beginners.*

*Customizable Templates: Tailor dispute letters for specific issues.*

*Educational Resources: Learn about credit reports and the dispute process.*

*Tracking: Monitor the status of disputes in real-time.*

*Cost-Effectiveness*

*Affordable Plans: Subscriptions typically range from $20 to $40 per month.*

*No Hidden Fees: Clear, transparent pricing.*

*Savings: Cheaper than traditional credit repair services.*

*Risk-Free Trials: Free trial periods or money-back guarantees available.*

*DisputeBee is an efficient and cost-effective solution for improving your credit score.*

# 14

## Chapter 14

REFRESH
Refresh.me helps improve credit scores and financial health easily and affordably. Here's how:

*Benefits*

1. **Credit Monitoring**: Real-time updates and alerts on credit scores and reports.
2. **Financial Tools**: Budgeting and debt management tools to track expenses and reduce debt.
3. **Personalized Advice**: Tailored tips and educational resources for credit improvement.
4. **User-Friendly**: Intuitive interface and mobile access for on-the-go management.

## Cost-Effectiveness

1. **Affordable Plans**: Subscriptions start around $10 to $20 per month.
2. **Transparent Pricing**: No hidden fees.
3. **Free Trials**: Risk-free trials and occasional discounts.

Refresh.me is an efficient and affordable solution for enhancing credit scores and financial health.

# Chapter 15

## IDENTITYIQ

IdentityIQ helps improve credit scores and financial health easily and affordably. Here's how:

*Benefits*

1. **Credit Monitoring**:

   - **Real-Time Alerts**: Provides real-time alerts for any changes in your credit report.
   - **Detailed Reports**: Regular access to comprehensive credit reports.

1. **Identity Theft Protection**:

   - **Fraud Alerts**: Monitors for signs of identity theft and alerts you immediately.
   - **Insurance**: Offers insurance to cover expenses related to

identity theft recovery.

1. **Financial Tools**:

- **Credit Score Tracker**: Tracks your credit score over time, helping you understand the impact of financial decisions.
- **Budgeting Tools**: Helps you create and manage budgets to improve financial health.

1. **User-Friendly**:

- **Easy Navigation**: Simple and intuitive interface for easy access to all features.
- **Mobile Access**: Manage your credit and financial health on the go.

## Cost-Effectiveness

1. **Affordable Plans**:

- **Low Monthly Fees**: Subscription plans typically start at around $10 to $30 per month.
- **Comprehensive Services**: Includes credit monitoring, identity theft protection, and financial tools.

1. **No Hidden Fees**:

- **Transparent Pricing**: Clear and straightforward pricing with no hidden costs.

1. **Free Trials and Discounts**:

## CHAPTER 15

- **Risk-Free Trials**: Many services offer free trial periods for new users.
- **Promotions**: Occasional discounts and promotions make the service even more affordable.

IdentityIQ is an efficient and affordable solution for improving your credit score and financial health, offering real-time credit monitoring, identity theft protection, financial tools, and a user-friendly interface.

# 16

# Chapter 16

Goddelyke Consulting

Goddelyke Consulting offers personalized credit and finance management services to help individuals achieve financial stability and improve their credit scores.

## *Services Offered*

1. **Credit Repair and Improvement**: They analyze credit reports, identify errors, and implement strategies to enhance credit profiles.
2. **Financial Planning**: Comprehensive financial planning tailored to manage income, expenses, and investments.
3. **Debt Management**: Solutions including consolidation, negotiation, and repayment plans to reduce debt burden.
4. **Budgeting and Saving**: Guidance on creating realistic budgets and saving strategies for a secure financial future.
5. **Education and Resources**: A library of articles, webinars, and workshops to help clients make informed financial

decisions.

*Why Choose Goddelyke Consulting?*

- **Expert Guidance**: Certified financial consultants provide tailored advice and support.
- **Personalized Approach**: Customized solutions for unique financial situations.

\* \* \*

- 

**Proven Results**: A strong track record in helping clients achieve financial stability and improve their credit scores.

- **Transparent Pricing**: Clear pricing with no hidden fees.

Goddelyke Consulting provides practical tools and knowledge to help clients take control of their financial future.

# 17

# Chapter 17

Government and Official Resources

1. **U.S. Department of Housing and Urban Development (HUD)**

- HUD.gov
- Provides comprehensive information about the Section 8 Homeownership Program, eligibility requirements, and how to find local PHAs.

1. **HUD Housing Choice Vouchers Fact Sheet**

- HUD Housing Choice Vouchers

1. **Find Your Local Public Housing Agency (PHA)**

## CHAPTER 17

- PHA Contact Information

1. **HUD Homeownership Vouchers Program**

- Homeownership Vouchers Program

*Homeownership Counseling and Financial Literacy*

1. **Consumer Financial Protection Bureau (CFPB)**

- CFPB.gov
- Offers tools and resources for financial literacy, budgeting, and homeownership.

1. **NeighborWorks America**

- NeighborWorks.org
- Provides homeownership counseling, financial education, and assistance programs.

1. **Habitat for Humanity**

- Habitat.org
- Offers affordable homeownership opportunities and homebuyer education programs.

*Finding a Home and Lender Resources*

1. **Zillow**

- Zillow.com

- A comprehensive real estate marketplace to search for homes and compare prices.

1. **Realtor.com**

- Realtor.com
- Offers property listings, real estate news, and resources for homebuyers.

1. **Bankrate**

- Bankrate.com
- Provides mortgage rate comparisons, lender reviews, and financial advice.

## Additional Resources and Assistance

1. **Local Initiatives Support Corporation (LISC)**

- LISC.org
- Offers support and funding for community development and affordable housing.

1. **Nolo**

- Nolo.com
- Provides legal information and guides on real estate transactions and homeownership.

1. **HUD Approved Housing Counseling Agencies**

CHAPTER 17

- HUD Approved Counselors
- Find HUD-approved housing counseling agencies in your area for personalized assistance.

*Down Payment Assistance Programs*

1. **Down Payment Resource**

- DownPaymentResource.com
- Connects homebuyers with down payment assistance programs and other resources.

1. **National Council of State Housing Agencies (NCSHA)**

- NCSHA.org
- Provides information on state housing finance agencies and their programs, including down payment assistance.

By utilizing these websites, you can access valuable information, resources, and support to help you navigate the process of buying a home with Section 8 assistance.

www.ingramcontent.com/pod-product-compliance
Lightning Source LLC
Chambersburg PA
CBHW072055230526
45479CB00010B/1091